Dear American Girl,

Friendship is a gift you give to yourself and to others. It's the best gift of all because it's totally personal and unique, just like you. No one else can be a friend in just the way you can.

But friendships don't happen overnight. They take time, patience, and hard work. A friendship is a little like riding a bicycle. Sometimes it's smooth and easy, sometimes bumpy and hilly. You have to pedal and steer to keep going straight, but it's usually worth the ride.

Some friendships last only a little while. Others may last a long time. But every friendship is a chance to learn more about yourself—and about how to be the best friend you can be. We hope the tips, quizzes, and activities in this book help you do just that!

Your friends at American Girl

AmericanGirl Library®

The Care and Keeping of Friends

Illustrated by Nadine Bernard Westcott

PLEASANT COMPANY PUBLICATIONS™

Published by Pleasant Company Publications
© 1996 by Pleasant Company

Printed in the United States of America.
98 99 00 KRH 10 9 8 7

American Girl Library® is a trademark of Pleasant Company.

Editorial Development: Andrea Weiss,
Michelle Watkins, Tamara England, Lynn Gordon
Art Direction: Kym Abrams
Design: Amy Nathan

Library of Congress Cataloguing-in-Publication Data
The care and keeping of friends / illustrated by Nadine Westcott. — 1st ed.
p. cm. — (American girl library)
Summary: Offers advice and activities for making friends,
being a friend, and celebrating friendship.
ISBN 1-56247-482-0
1. Friendship—Juvenile literature. [1. Friendship.]
I. Westcott, Nadine Bernard, ill.
II. Series: American girl library (Middleton, Wis.)
BF575.F66C36 1996
158'.25—dc20   96-11549   CIP   AC

Making Friends

There's nothing wrong with doing things by yourself, but some things are just more fun with a friend. It takes time, patience, and a little luck to find the right person and get a friendship off the ground.

How can I find a friend?

KNOWING WHERE to LOOK

Sometimes it just takes being in the right place at the right time to find a friend. Get involved in activities you enjoy, and you'll improve your chances of meeting someone to enjoy them with. Keep your eyes open the next time you're . . .

EATING LUNCH

The school cafeteria is a great place to meet girls from other homerooms or grade levels.

TAKING A CLASS

Whether you take Intermediate Skating or How to Make Bead Jewelry, you'll meet girls with similar interests and talents.

Visiting the Library

Of course, you'll have to whisper hello or pass notes to introduce yourselves!

Going to Camp

Camp friends make great pen pals even after the summer is over.

VOLUNTEERING

Sign up at a recycling center, animal shelter, or nursing home. If you care about others, you're bound to meet people who care about you.

Joining a Club

In Girl Scouts, 4-H, and other after-school groups, you'll work on projects together and find friends who can help you reach your own goals.

Playing a Sport

Join the team! Regular practices and exciting games can lead to close friendships.

5

Making the First Move

Just act natural! Be yourself! You've probably heard that advice a million times and thought, "That's easy for you to say!" You're right. The truth is, it's hard to feel totally relaxed and comfortable with someone you hardly know. But you can become confident enough to make the first move.

Remember

⇨ The person you approach might feel just as shy and nervous as you do—maybe more!

⇨ Most people are flattered when someone shows interest in them. It's hard not to like a person who likes you.

⇨ If someone isn't interested in getting to know you, it's that person's loss, not yours.

CAUTION:
Shyness can often
be mistaken for
unfriendliness.

6 Conversation Starters

Before you lose your nerve, take the first step with one of these openers:

Want me to help you with that?

1 Be on the lookout for opportunities to help out. Perhaps you can lend a hand with an armload of books, or help set up props for an oral report.

Your locker looks so cool!

2 Give a compliment. It's one of the easiest ways to get someone's attention. Does this person have a cute new haircut? Does she write great stories? Tell her! She'll be flattered.

I was wondering if you could show me...

3 Is this person good at something you're trying to learn, such as how to multiply fractions or make a French braid? When asked in just the right way, people are usually eager to show what they know.

Where did you get all those pins?

4 Show interest in somebody's hobbies. Everyone likes a chance to talk about their favorite activity, whether it's sticker trading or tap dancing.

Do you want to eat lunch together?

6 An invitation is a great way to get to the point quickly. Are you having a birthday party? Looking for an after-school playmate or a field-trip buddy? Just come right out and ask—it's easier than you think!

I hope it keeps snowing!

5 The weather is one of the most popular things to talk about. That's because it's easy—everybody knows about it, and everybody has to live with it. Don't be afraid to fall back on this old conversation standby.

OtHeR IDeAs

Talk about a movie.

Tell a joke.

Ask for directions.

Discuss a class project.

9

Choosing Carefully

That girl seems nice. I wonder if we could be friends.

It's hard to know who's a good match for you. Not all people are perfect together, no matter how nice they are or how much they have in common. You probably know from past experience how long it takes to feel really comfortable with someone. That's because it takes time to get to know a person and to find out if the seed of friendship is going to grow.

✦ Remember ✦

When you're getting to know someone, ask these things:

✿ **How interested is the person in making new friends?**
Does she go out of her way to include new people, or does she act like she's already got enough friends?

✿ **How often do you see the person?**
Will it be easy or hard for you to get together? Are you looking for a neighborhood buddy or would you consider a long-distance pen pal?

✿ **Are you judging the person too quickly?**
People can surprise you. Sometimes friendships you think will be great don't go anywhere. And other times someone you almost pass by turns out to be the best pal ever.

Quiz
How Do You Know Who's Right for You?

When it comes to choosing close friends, some reasons *are* better than others. Think about the person you'd like to be friends with. Then check the top five things on the list below that describe her or him.

This person . . .

☐ **1.** is always kind to people.

☐ **2.** is really cute.

☐ **3.** is friendly to me.

☐ **4.** is popular.

☐ **5.** has the same interests as I do.

☐ **6.** always knows the latest gossip.

☐ **7.** is honest.

☐ **8.** has big slumber parties.

Hi!

□ 9. always keeps her promise.

□ 10. has lots of games to play with.

□ 11. seems interested in getting to know me.

□ 12. always wears clothes that are in style.

What did you check?

If you checked mostly odd-numbered answers, you've picked someone with the special qualities it takes to be a true, trustworthy friend.

If you checked mostly the even-numbered answers, you may want to look deeper before deciding whether this person will be a caring friend to you.

Remember: A person's looks or the things she owns don't guarantee that she'll treat you well or like you for who you are.

Could I help? I love building sandcastles!

Alone but Not Lonely

No matter how many friends you have, or how good you are at making new friends, you still have to be by yourself sometimes.
So get to know yourself better, learn to enjoy your own company, and make the most of your time alone. Nobody can be a better friend to you than YOU!

10 Things to Do by Yourself

1. Write a fan letter.
2. Teach yourself a magic trick.
3. Go to the library for books, music, and more!
4. Prepare a special meal for your family.
5. Do volunteer work.
6. Start a diary and write in it regularly.
7. Invent a new dance.
8. Practice shooting baskets or jumping rope.
9. Reorganize your closet.
10. Write a song.

BEING A FRIEND

The best part about being friends is that the more you give, the more you get back. Remember: The only way to have a friend is to be one.

About "Best" Friends

Everyone likes to feel special. So it may seem important to be someone's *best* friend, and to let everyone know who *your* best friend is. But when you single out one person, you may miss opportunities with other girls—and boys—who could be great friends. So instead of trying to decide who's at the top of your list, and worrying about whether you're at the top of your friend's, just concentrate on being a good friend to *everyone* you care about.

Remember

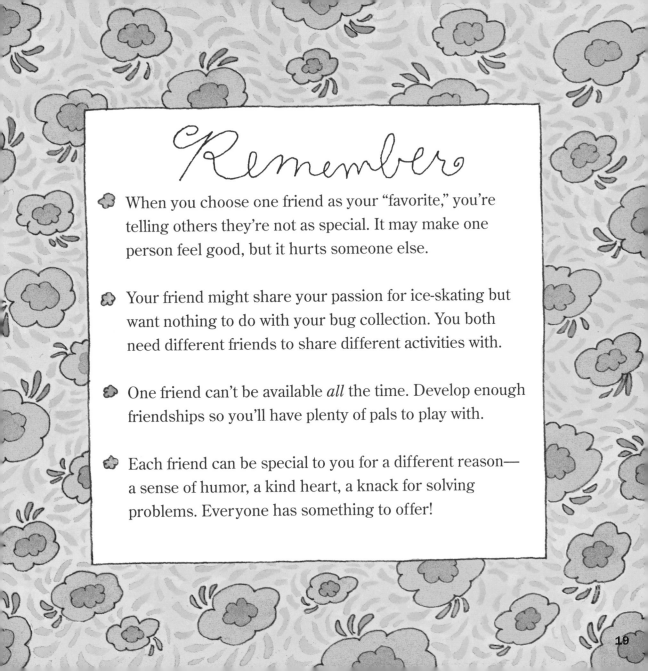

- When you choose one friend as your "favorite," you're telling others they're not as special. It may make one person feel good, but it hurts someone else.

- Your friend might share your passion for ice-skating but want nothing to do with your bug collection. You both need different friends to share different activities with.

- One friend can't be available *all* the time. Develop enough friendships so you'll have plenty of pals to play with.

- Each friend can be special to you for a different reason— a sense of humor, a kind heart, a knack for solving problems. Everyone has something to offer!

Quiz
Famous Fictional Friends

Friendships come in all shapes and sizes. Who could ever forget
Pooh and Piglet, Snoopy and Woodstock, or even Snow White and
the Seven Dwarfs? They all knew the true meaning of friendship.
Test your knowledge of famous friends. Match each pair or group
of characters with the book or movie in which they appeared.

1. Charlotte and Wilbur

2. Henry and Beezus

3. The March sisters

4. Simba and Nala

5. Mary Lennox, Dickon, and Colin

6. Samantha and Nellie

7. Gilly, Trotter, and William Ernest

8. Kristy, Claudia, Dawn, Mallory, Mary Anne, Stacey, and Jessica

9. Nancy, Bess, and George

a. *Little Women*

b. the Baby-Sitters Club books

c. *The Great Gilly Hopkins*

d. the Ramona books

e. the Nancy Drew mysteries

f. *Charlotte's Web*

g. *The Secret Garden*

h. The American Girls Collection® Samantha books

i. *The Lion King*

Answers

ALIKE BUT DIFFERENT

Some friends are mirror images of each other. They get along great because they're exactly alike. Others are complete opposites. They enjoy each other, even though they seem to have nothing in common. But most good friends are both alike *and* different. Being similar makes it easy to understand each other and spend time together. Being different makes the friendship interesting—and fun!

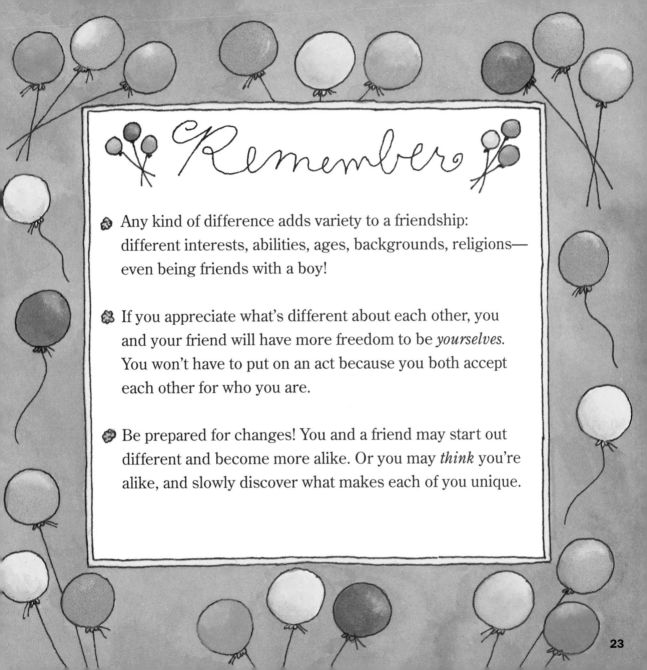

Remember

- Any kind of difference adds variety to a friendship: different interests, abilities, ages, backgrounds, religions— even being friends with a boy!

- If you appreciate what's different about each other, you and your friend will have more freedom to be *yourselves*. You won't have to put on an act because you both accept each other for who you are.

- Be prepared for changes! You and a friend may start out different and become more alike. Or you may *think* you're alike, and slowly discover what makes each of you unique.

What's the Difference?

Friends who are different from you can still be true-blue buddies. Here are six great reasons to be glad for the things that set you and your friends apart.

DEVELOPING NEW INTERESTS

1 By learning about your friend's interests, you may discover new ones of your own. Perhaps you didn't think fossil hunting or folk dancing could be fun!

What's the capital of Ohio?

Making New Friends

3 By participating in different activities, you and your friend will get to know different people. Introduce her to your swimming buddies in return for meeting her scout troop.

Teaching and Learning

2 Your friend is great at sports but terrified of tests. You're prepared for every pop quiz but get tired just thinking about gym class. When you have different skills, you can share what you know and coach each other.

GETTING a BOY'S POINT of VIEW

5 You can learn a lot by being friends with a boy. Boys and girls are often treated differently, and that makes them think and act differently. Find out how he feels about the new art teacher or who he thinks should be team captain. His answers may surprise you!

IGNORING THE AGE DIFFERENCE

4 It's important to have friends your own age, but spending time with younger or older people can also be fun. It's probably easier to tell a younger friend that you're afraid of the dark. With an older friend, you can feel more grown-up when she lets you try on her clothes or read her secret diary.

Taking a Break

6 Even the closest friends need time apart. Having your own interests and activities will keep you from getting sick of each other.

25

Quiz

How Well Do You Know Each Other?

There's always more to learn about a friend. On separate pieces of paper, you and your friend should each write the answers you think the other would give below. Then switch papers and see how many you got right.

1. If there's one food your friend despises, it's ____.
2. If there's one food your friend would eat every day, it's ____.
3. Your friend's favorite song is ____.
4. A song that drives your friend nuts is ____.
5. The person your friend would most like to spend the day with is ____.
6. Which does your friend have the most of?
   a. leotards
   b. baseball caps
   c. miniskirts

7. The thing your friend likes the most about you is ____.
8. The thing your friend would probably change about you is ____.

9. Your friend dreams of
    a. competing in the Olympics.
    b. flying on the space shuttle.
    c. teaching at your school.

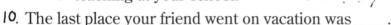

10. The last place your friend went on vacation was ____.
11. The place your friend hopes to go someday is ____.
12. Your friend's favorite subject in school is ____.
13. The subject that gives your friend nightmares is ____.
14. The thing your friend would *least* like to do is
    a. eat a liver-and-peanut-butter sandwich.
    b. sing a solo in front of 500 people.
    c. pet a worm.

How did you do?

Give yourself a point for each answer that you got right. If you matched . . .

11 or more: You can practically read your friend's mind!

7–10: You two are *closerthanthis*, but you can still be surprised sometimes.

6 or fewer: Your friendship is growing. You're learning new things all the time.

FARAWAY FRIENDS

Being separated from someone you really care about can test even the closest of friendships. Whatever the distance—across town or across the country—it can feel like a million miles. Suddenly there's a huge hole in your life, and you feel sad, angry, and lonely.

Change is painful and scary. But it's a part of life. You can't always know who will come or go, but you can grow from the experience.

Remember

🌀 Try not to feel angry if your friend has to move. It's not her fault. As she's preparing to leave, she may appear to be caught up in the excitement and not have much time for you. But that doesn't mean she doesn't care.

🌀 Don't forget about all the other people who care about you—family, neighbors, other friends, even teachers. Spending time with them can't replace your friend, but it can help fill the emptiness you feel.

🌀 If you're the one moving, focus on all the great things that await you in your new home. Share your excitement with your friend, and make sure she knows how much you wish she were coming along!

5 WAYS to STAY CLOSE

Just because you're far apart doesn't mean you have to grow apart.
Try these creative ways to keep in touch.

Funky Junk from Far Away

2 Send each other ticket stubs, matchbooks, take-out menus, or other mementos from all the places you go. If your friend lives in a different country, ask her to send you coins, stamps, or even gum wrappers for a really unique collection.

A Thoughtful Hello

1 Pick a time of day to close your eyes and think of each other. It could be a wake-up call, a good-night hug, or a midday hello. Just remember: If you live in different time zones, you'll have to synchronize your schedules.

"ME TOO" DAY

3 Once a week, arrange to do the same activity on the same day, such as seeing a particular movie or playing a certain sport. Afterward, write a letter or an e-mail message to each other about what you liked and didn't like.

TELL-ALL TAPES

4 There's nothing like hearing each other's voice—but don't stop there. Record the sounds you used to experience together: the class picnic, your piano recital, a trip to the beach. Ask your friend to tape her new surroundings and introduce you to her new friends.

Traveling Tale

5 Start by writing the beginning of a story and sending or e-mailing it to your friend. Then have her add a few more sentences and send it back. Keep sending it back and forth. See how silly you can make the story and how long you can keep it going!

Telephone Tips

Always ask your parents before calling. Find out when it will cost the least (usually nights and weekends).

Write down ahead of time what you want to say so you don't forget a thing!

Put a time limit on your conversation, and stick to it.

Arrange to call at a certain time so your friend can plan to be home. Then you won't have to pay for missed calls.

Make a Smiles-Across-the-Miles Calendar

Special friendships can survive time and distance. Fill up each month with her smiling face, and you'll feel like you're experiencing the seasons together!

Each of you should make your own calendar.

You Will Both Need:

- ⭐ Piece of poster board or heavy craft paper, 22 inches by 28 inches
- ⭐ Yardstick
- ⭐ Pencil and markers
- ⭐ Calendar showing the next 12 months
- ⭐ Glue or tape
- ⭐ Thumbtacks
- ⭐ Camera and film

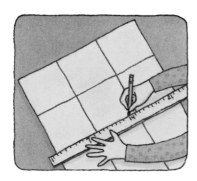

1 Use the yardstick and pencil to divide the poster into 12 boxes, each 7 inches tall and a little more than 7 inches wide.

2 In the boxes, write the names of the months, starting with the month you and your friend were (or will be) parted.

3 Fill in the days and dates for each month by copying them from a real calendar. Or glue or tape the actual calendar page in each square if it fits.

4 Find a place where you have permission to hang the poster with tacks. If you can't put holes in walls or doors, see if you can hang it from a bulletin board.

5 Throughout each month, each of you should have pictures taken of yourself doing different things and celebrating special events. At the end of the month, send your pictures to each other.

6 When you receive your friend's pictures, tape or glue them onto the month in which they were taken. By the end of the year, each of you will have filled the other's poster with happy memories!

LENDING A HAND

Don't worry, I'll help you!

We all go through hard times—school struggles, family problems, sickness, or just plain bad days. No matter how big or small, a problem can feel like the end of the world. But anything's easier to face when you don't have to face it alone—and that's what friends are for! You may not be able to fix your friend's bike, or find her lost puppy, or soothe her stomachache, but you can help in simple ways.

Remember

☐ Sometimes a smile or kind word is all it takes to make someone feel better. Admire her art project, compliment her outfit, or just hug her and say, "I'm glad we're friends."

☐ Be a good listener. Talking about a problem can often help someone sort out confusing feelings or just let off steam.

☐ Try not to judge your friend, even if you don't agree with how she's handling the problem. No situation is as simple as it seems.

☐ If your friend's problem is really bad, such as a serious illness or family tragedy, it may take a lot of her attention away from you. You'll have to be extra understanding.

6 Ways to Show You Care

Got a friend who's hit some bumps and is down in the dumps?
Try one of these pick-me-ups.

"♡"

Favor Coupons

2 Present your friend with a book of coupons to cash in for different favors— the use of your bicycle, a free hair braiding, or whatever your friend needs the most.

1 FREE PICNIC for 1 day

My bike for 1 day

1 free hair braiding

Cheer up Powwow

1 Call an emergency get-together of your friend's closest pals and relatives, and deliver a group hug. Shower your friend with kindness, happy thoughts, and support.

"Ode" of Admiration

3 Lift your friend's spirits with a special poem or song about all of her great qualities.

First-Aid Fun Kit

4 Gather funky hair accessories, colorful school supplies, silly pictures of you, sweet treats, and other items guaranteed to bring a smile to her face.

Queen for a Day

5 Give your friend the royal treatment at school. Carry her books, clean up her lunch tray, give her the first turn at everything—wait on her hand and foot!

CHORE BREAK

6 Is your friend feeling overwhelmed by responsibilities in and out of school? Maybe you can lend a hand with her chores— making beds, doing dishes, raking the leaves.

Make a Feel-Better Yarn Doll

Give your friend around-the-clock comfort with this squeezable mini version of you. It lets her know you'll always be there for her, even when you can't be with her.

You Will Need:

- ♥ 12 yards of yarn
- ♥ Piece of cardboard, 7 inches by 5 inches
- ♥ 7 pieces of yarn, each 5 inches long
- ♥ Scissors
- ♥ Styrofoam® or rubber ball, 1 inch wide
- ♥ Fabric glue
- ♥ 3 buttons, 2 of them about the same color as your eyes
- ♥ Bits of yarn about the same color as your hair

1 Wrap the yards of yarn around the cardboard the long way. Slip a short piece of yarn under the wrapped yarn at the top. Tie it together tightly with a double knot. Cut the yarn open at the bottom of the cardboard.

2 Place the yarn over the small ball. Arrange so it covers the ball completely. Use another short piece of yarn to tie the yarn together at the bottom of the ball. Divide the rest of the yarn into four equal sections.

3 To make the arms, take the two outer sections and tie each of them about halfway down with a short piece of yarn. Cut off the yarn that remains below the ties.

4 To make the body, put the two middle sections together and tie them about 1/3 of the way down with a short piece of yarn.

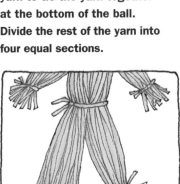

5 Make the legs by tying each remaining section at the bottom with a short piece of yarn.

6 Trim off all of the loose ends of yarn near the knots where you tied things together. Glue on the buttons for two eyes and a nose. Then glue on a yarn smile and hair.

Quiz
STEP IN or Stay Out?

When a friend is having trouble, it's natural to want to help. But do you know the difference between *helping* and *interfering*? Decide how you would handle each situation below.

 Your friend has been getting bad grades lately. Her parents will ground her if they don't improve. You . . .

a. Let her copy off your A+ papers until things blow over.

b. Offer to study with her and go over the things she doesn't understand.

c. Mind your own business. If she gets bad grades, it's her own fault.

 Your friend has been acting quieter than usual. You're really worried, but she insists nothing's wrong. You . . .

a. Keep pestering her. You're dying to know what's going on, and you're a little angry that she won't open up.

b. Make sure she knows you're there if she needs you; then drop the subject. If you're really concerned, talk to an adult.

c. Let her sulk. Stay away until she's in a better mood.

3 Your friend is fuming about a fight she just had with someone else. Deep down, you think it may be her fault. You . . .

a. Rush to defend her anyway. Go tell the other person no one treats your friend like that and gets away with it!

b. Let her talk about how upset she is, but don't take sides in the fight.

c. Tell her you don't want to hear about it. She brought it on herself!

4 Your friend's cat had to be put to sleep. She's so sad she can't stop crying. You . . .

a. Tell her to go out and get another cat. She should forget about her pet as soon as possible.

b. Tell her how sorry you are. Invite her to come over and play with your cat anytime.

c. Tell her to stop moping around. It was just an animal!

How did you do?

Look at your answers. If you picked *b* most of the time, you're a good judge of situations. You know that you can't solve a friend's problems, but you *can* lend a hand—or even a shoulder to cry on—when the going gets tough.

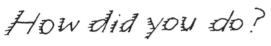

TROUBLE!

Even good friends fight. Friendships can change, and friends sometimes grow apart. You probably know all that. But do you know what to do when it happens to you?

43

FEARSOME FIGHTS

Whether it's a screaming match or the silent treatment, a fight isn't fun for anyone. A silly misunderstanding can turn into a big blowup and make you forget why you ever became friends in the first place! But everyone argues sometimes—even good friends. Understanding why you're fighting, and knowing how to fight fair, can mean the difference between making up and breaking up.

Remember

🌧 Don't argue just to prove a point. Know the difference between sharing important feelings and dragging out a silly disagreement.

🌧 Sometimes people take their problems out on their friends without realizing it. Think about why you're fighting: Are you really mad at each other, or could something else be bothering one of you?

🌧 Don't get stuck in the middle of other people's fights, even if you think you're the best person to solve the disagreement. Ask your friends not to pull you into their arguments with each other.

7 Top Trouble Starters

Friends get into sticky situations with each other all the time. Just knowing the most common reasons friends fight can help you stop arguments before they start. Recognize any of these troublemakers?

Queen Bee
bosses her friends around and tries to control everything.

Tug O' Warrior
forces a friend to choose between her and another friend.

Back-Out
makes promises and then doesn't follow through.

BYE!

BIG MOUTH
shares a friend's top-secret news to impress others.

Show-Off
points out how much better she is than everyone else.

Terrible Two-Face
talks about friends behind their backs.

JOKER
thinks teasing her friends is funny—even when they don't.

47

Do You Know How to Fight Fair?

Sometimes you can't avoid a fight. But do you know how to fight fair? Read each fighting strategy and decide whether it's fair or unfair by circling your choice. You make the call!

1. When you're arguing, if you talk really loudly and even cry, you'll always get your point across better.

2. Talk to everyone about the problem except your friend. Get lots of people on your side so your friend will give in faster.

3. Don't be too specific about why you're angry. Your friend should already know why you're mad.

4. When your friend is talking, don't concentrate on what she's saying. Instead, plan what to say next.

5. Make sure you bring up everything your friend's ever done that bothers you—not just what you're unhappy about now.

6. The silent treatment is better than arguing. A cold shoulder will cause your friend to warm up fast!

Now turn the page to find out whether you can call yourself a fair fighter!

HOW DID YOU ANSWER?

Did you call a foul on every strategy listed on the last two pages? The pros who know say they're all unfair ways to fight. Here are ground rules every girl should know about fighting fair.

Cool it.

PRIVATE— KEEP OTHERS OUT.

Name the problem.

1 Shouts or tears will get a person's attention, but they also keep that person from understanding the real reason you're upset. Try to express yourself as calmly as you can. Remember, words said in anger can *really* hurt.

2 Talking to others can help you sort out your feelings, but it's no substitute for talking directly to the person you're mad at. Don't put others in the middle.

3 Don't expect your friend to read your mind. She can't change or fix the problem if she doesn't know what it is.

4 It's hard to listen when you're angry. But your friend may be trying to tell you something important that could change how you feel. If you hear it soon enough, you can often stop a fight before it gets worse.

5 Bringing up things from the past or starting up old arguments takes everyone's attention away from what's happening now.

6 Some people deal with arguments by changing the subject or trying to pretend there isn't a problem. Ignoring the problem—or your friend—won't make things better.

MAKING IT BETTER

No matter how it starts, and no matter how silly or serious it gets, a disagreement can be fixed. Knowing how to listen and talk—even when you're both really upset—will not only save your friendship but make it stronger.

Remember

❊ Don't be afraid to make the first move. It doesn't mean you're letting your friend "win." It just means you care enough to work things out. Neither of you wins if you never speak again!

❊ Adults can help. Sometimes a person with an outside view can help you see things more clearly. You may want to talk to a school counselor. That's why he or she is there.

❊ Keep your sense of humor. Can the two of you together find anything funny about what happened? Laughing at the situation (not at each other) can make things feel more comfortable.

8 GREAT ICE BREAKERS

A bad fight can build a wall of ice between friends. Take the first step toward melting it down by giving one of these gifts and its meaningful message.

1. It was a mistake. Can we start over?

2. Can we make it better?

3. Let's find a way to stick together!

5. This bubble hasn't burst yet!

4. We can save this friendship!

6. Let's not write this friendship off!

7. I know we can be buds again!

To my "bud"

8. We're still friends at the core.

SAYING YOU'RE SORRY

Sometimes the best way to break the ice is with an apology—but only if it's sincere. NEVER say you're sorry unless you mean it. If you're just trying to end a fight, your true feelings are sure to slip out later. But if you *are* wrong, admit it loud and clear—with words that get to the heart of the matter.

Remember: Don't be too proud to ask for forgiveness—or too stubborn to give it!

I didn't mean to hurt you.

I wish I hadn't said that.

I think I made a mistake.

I should have told you sooner.

6 Tips for Talking It Out

Are you ready to hear each other out? If so, all you need are a quiet place and the willingness to work together. Remember these helpful hints.

1 The more you listen to your friend, the more she'll want to listen to you. Agree to take turns talking so you both get a chance to say what's on your mind.

I guess I was feeling left out.

3 Try to understand the other person's feelings. You know how *you* feel, but put yourself in your friend's shoes. Why might she have acted the way she did?

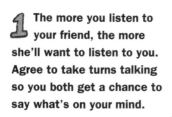

Thanks for listening.

2 Describe your own feelings instead of telling your friend what she did wrong.

I never thought of it like that!

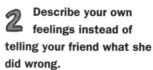

5 Try to avoid saying *always* or *never*. It's probably not true, and it will just get your friend angry.

6 You can agree to disagree. You might both be sorry about what happened and still not agree on everything.

4 Make an agreement about how to handle things in the future. Maybe you've each learned that you'd rather hear the truth— as long as it's said the right way—than be kept in the dark.

Make a Back-Together Bracelet

Tell your pal, "This friendship is *knot* over!" Let her know the ties are just as strong as ever.

You Will Need:

★ Scissors

★ 24 inches of yarn or thick cord—multicolored yarn looks best

★ Ruler

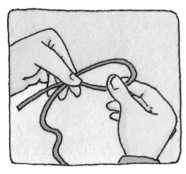

1 Cut a 24-inch piece of yarn. Fold the end over about 3 inches to make a loop. Pinch the base of the loop tightly together.

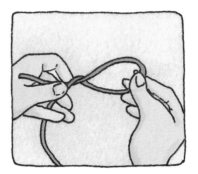

2 Twist the loop around one full turn, still pinching the base tightly.

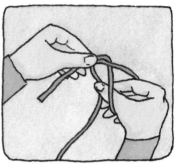

3 Start your bracelet by reaching through the loop and pulling the yarn through to make a new loop.

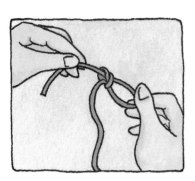

4 Hold the loop with one hand. With your other hand, pull on the short tail of the yarn to make a knot.

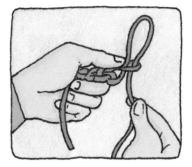

5 Continue making loops by bringing the yarn through the last loop and pulling on the tail to tighten. To make the loop smaller, pull the long end of the yarn.

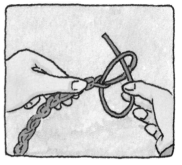

6 When your bracelet's long enough, bring the end of the yarn up through the last loop to make a knot. Cut the yarn, leaving enough at the ends to tie the bracelet around your friend's wrist.

FRIENDS FOREVER? NOT ALWAYS

When a friendship begins to fade, it doesn't necessarily mean that one of you has done something wrong or has become a bad person. The sad truth is that some friendships don't last forever.

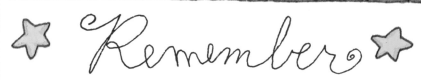

Remember

Friendships can change for lots of reasons. For instance:

⭐ **New interests.** You used to do everything together. Now she wants to play with her dolls and you're into soccer.

⭐ **Being apart.** Moving away or being in different classes doesn't have to end a friendship, but things will change.

⭐ **Family life.** A new baby, a visiting grandparent, or a divorce can affect relationships outside your family.

⭐ **New friends.** If you're spending a lot of time with other people and not much time with each other, you may start to grow apart.

Quiz
Can This Friendship Be Saved?

If you have a friendship that seems to be floundering, read on! Check the statements that apply to you and your friend. Then read the answers and decide for yourself if the friendship can be rescued.

☐ **1.** You always find yourself playing by your friend's rules—or not playing at all.

☐ **2.** You've been avoiding your friend, thinking up just about any excuse not to be around her.

☐ **3.** You feel "used" by your friend.

☐ **4.** You don't have any of the same interests as your friend. It's been hard finding *anything* to do together or even to talk about.

No, sorry, I can't come over today. I have to clean the goldfish bowl.

☐ **5.** Your friend is pressuring you to do things you don't want to do, like lying or even stealing.

☐ **6.** All you can see are the differences between you and your friend—not the similarities.

☐ **7.** Your friend keeps hurting your feelings with insults disguised as "joking."

☐ **8.** When you're together, you find yourself focusing on what's wrong with your friend.

How did you answer?

If you checked mostly even-numbered statements . . .

Ask yourself a hard question: Do you really want to save this friendship? It sounds like you're drifting away. Be honest with your friend. If you want more time to yourself, tell her so. That way she can spend time with others who'll be glad for her friendship.

If you checked mostly odd-numbered statements . . .

The only way to save this friendship is to stand up for yourself! Make it clear that your friend has to treat you with respect. If she really cares, she'll change her ways. If not, don't waste your time with someone who hurts your feelings over and over.

If you checked even *and* odd statements . . .

It's possible both of you are ready to let go of this friendship. It's time to talk—now.

Looking Ahead

Every friendship you have, no matter how long it lasts, is a learning experience. It teaches you about yourself and other people, and it helps you become a better friend. So even when a friendship has ended, there's something to look forward to—the great new friendship that may be waiting for you just around the corner!

Remember

Whether you're patching up a friendship or realizing you need to let go of one, think about what's in the word *friends* itself:

F riends are people who accept you for YOU.

R emember to let them be themselves, too!

I t's not always easy to get along—

E ven with close friends, things can go wrong.

N ow, friendships may fade, but keep in mind . . .

D eep in your heart, you'll always find, there's

S ome part of each friend you can't leave behind.

Celebrating Friendship

A good friendship is something to cheer about! You can celebrate it on special days and every day—just by being together, sharing good times, and surprising each other with little reminders of how much you care.

Here's to us!

Friends 'til the end!

Anyday Activities
7 WAYS to beat the BOREDOM BLUES

What do you do when there's nothing to do? Try one of these activities.

TALK SHOW

1 Take turns hosting a pretend talk show and interviewing each other.

ON THE AIR

Name Game

2 Think up new names for yourselves, family members, even pets. They can be silly or sweet, but you have to use them all day long!

CRAZY CONVERSATIONS

3 Have a conversation without using the letter T. Or try using only words with just one syllable. See how long you can go!

Catalogue Shopping

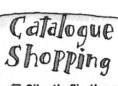

4 Silently flip through a catalogue together, each of you making a secret list of the things you'd like to buy. Then try to guess what's on each other's lists.

5 Pick actors for a movie based on a book you've read. Who would play each character? Choose your favorite stars, people you know, or even yourselves!

COMMERCIAL BREAK

6 Make up silly TV commercials about real or make-believe products. Then act out the ads.

Silly Swap Day

7 One day a week, swap a sock or another piece of clothing with your friend and wear it for the whole day!

Anyday Activities, continued

Always Room for More!

Here are ideas for you and one friend, two friends, three, or more.
Each new person adds to the fun!

Games for 2

Back Talk

Take turns "writing" messages on each other's backs with your fingers and trying to figure out what the message is.

Mirror Game

Stand or sit face to face. Pick a leader. The leader slowly moves her arms or legs while the other tries to mirror the movements exactly. See how in sync you can be!

Games for 3

Gold, Silver, Bronze

Compete for first, second, and third place in crazy competitions such as great big bubble blowing or shoelace speed tying.

Triple Tap

Two people sit back to back. The third person calls out a color. The sitting players must run and find three different things of that color and tap each thing three times. The first one back to the starting point becomes the caller.

Games for 4 or more

MELT TAG

Instead of freeze tag, play a game where you melt on the ground when you're tagged. You can become "solid" again if another player pulls you up.

JUNIOR ACADEMY AWARDS

It's up to you to choose! Vote on Best Movie, Best Song, Best Animal Character, etc. Then celebrate by eating the Best Ice Cream Flavor!

Make a Time Capsule

Mark the first day of winter, the last day of school, or any special event by collecting friendship memories and storing them in a time capsule. Whether you bring it out six months or six years later, it'll take you right back to today!

You Will Need:

- A large sturdy box, plastic container, or can with a lid
- Writing paper
- Pens or markers
- Packing tape

1 Gather photos, letters, ticket stubs, or other mementos from the fun times you and your friends have had throughout the year. Place the items in the container.

2 Have each person write a description of her favorite memory from the year, along with a prediction for the future. Fold up everyone's papers and put them in the container.

3 Make an *inventory*, or list, of everything you put in your time capsule and why. Have everybody sign and date the paper. Then fold it up and place it in the container.

4 Seal the container with the packing tape. On the lid, write today's date and the date the capsule is to be opened.

5 Find a spot to store the capsule—perhaps hidden in the back of a closet or on a shelf in the basement, attic, or garage. Just be sure the capsule will stay safe and dry.

6 Now try to forget about your time capsule until it's time to open it!

Made for Each Other
Homemade Friendship Tokens

A gift from the heart doesn't have to be store-bought. Try one of these easy-to-make tokens.

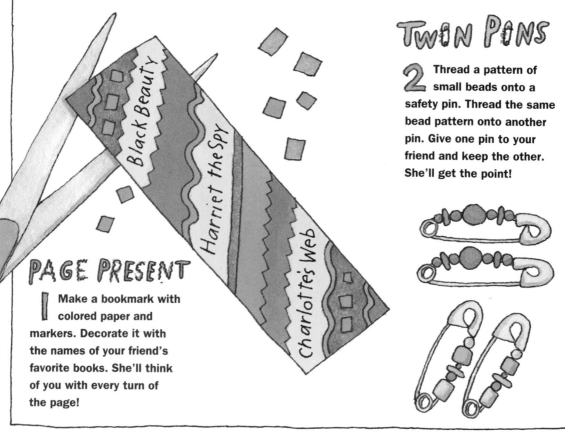

TWIN PINS

2 Thread a pattern of small beads onto a safety pin. Thread the same bead pattern onto another pin. Give one pin to your friend and keep the other. She'll get the point!

PAGE PRESENT

1 Make a bookmark with colored paper and markers. Decorate it with the names of your friend's favorite books. She'll think of you with every turn of the page!

Lovely Laces

3 Your friend will get a kick out of personalized shoelaces! Use waterproof markers to write her name or initials on plain white laces. Decorate the laces with her favorite colors.

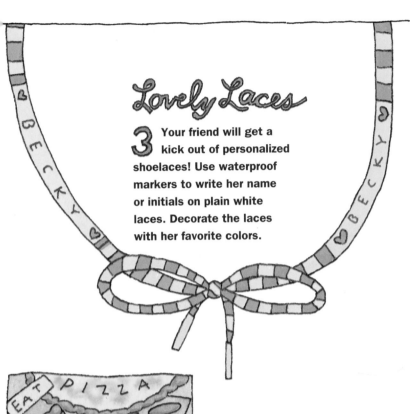

Keepsake Collage

4 What does your friend love more than anything else? Horses? Seashells? Pizza? Cut out pictures and words from old magazines and make a collage about her favorite thing.

Surprise!

A gift is twice as nice when it appears out of nowhere! Sneak up with one of these:

Half-Birthday Card

Six months from your friend's birthday, send her a card that says: "*Half* a nice *half-birthday*. In *half* a year, we'll *half* a great time!"

Funny Face

Enlarge a photo of yourself on a photocopy machine. Write a silly message on it and hide it in her locker—or even under her pillow, if you can!

Hidden Hellos

Write little messages on sticky notes and stick them in your friend's notebook, on the inside of her desktop, or other surprising places.

Make a Pal Pen

Let your friend know you'll always be "write" within reach!

You Will Need:

- Scissors
- 2 colors of embroidery floss
- Ruler
- Craft glue
- Tape
- Ballpoint pen
- Beads or charms

1 Cut a piece of embroidery floss 4 inches long. Tie a double knot near one end. Dab a bit of glue at the other end and twist into a point. Let dry.

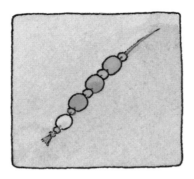

2 String beads or charms onto the floss. The hardened tip will make this easier.

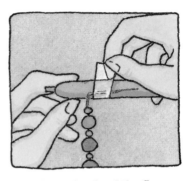

3 Tape the tip of the floss to the end of the pen that is opposite the writing end.

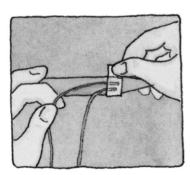

4 Cut 2 different-colored pieces of floss about 5 feet long. Tape the ends next to each other at the writing end of the pen, where the pointed part becomes straight.

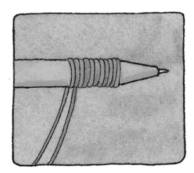

5 Wrap the 2 pieces of floss tightly around the pen, covering the piece of tape. Keep wrapping all the way up until you've covered the tape at the other end, too.

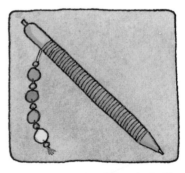

6 Use a dab of glue to hold the floss in place at the end. Trim off any extra floss. Let dry. Then wrap up your pen and present it to your pal!

MakE BUDdY bon~Bons

Give your friend some tasty chocolate–peanut butter treats that are just like the two of you. Alone, both flavors are great, but together they're truly terrific!

You Will Need:

- 2 cups powdered sugar
- 1 cup graham cracker crumbs
- 1/2 cup (1 stick) margarine
- 1/2 cup creamy peanut butter
- 1 1/2 cups semisweet chocolate chips
- 3 tablespoons shortening
- Measuring cups and spoons
- Mixing spoon and mixing bowl
- Saucepan or microwavable bowl
- Paper towel
- Cookie sheet and aluminum foil
- Plastic wrap
- Small, deep bowl
- Toothpicks

Have an adult help you with Steps 2 and 5!

1 In the mixing bowl, combine the powdered sugar and graham cracker crumbs.

2 Melt the margarine and peanut butter in a saucepan on the stove. Or microwave on HIGH for 1 minute in a microwavable bowl covered with a paper towel. Stir.

3 Mix the peanut butter mixture with the graham cracker-sugar mixture. This will make a crumbly dough.

4 Make balls of dough by using about 1 teaspoon of dough at a time and rolling it in the palm of your hand. Place the balls on a cookie sheet lined with foil.

5 Melt the chocolate chips and shortening in a saucepan on the stove. Or microwave them on HIGH in a microwavable bowl covered with plastic wrap for about 3 minutes, stopping every minute to stir.

6 Pour the mixture into the small, deep bowl. Use a toothpick to dip the balls halfway into the chocolate, then set them on their sides on the cookie sheet. Take out the toothpick. Put the bonbons in the refrigerator to cool.

Party Time!
"Puzzling" Invitations

Why wait for a birthday or holiday to get together? Have a "Just Because We're Friends" party—you can all be the guests of honor!

On the front of the card...

Create a word search that contains all the guests' names. Draw a big square and write each name inside, going across, down, or diagonally. Fill in other letters around the names to make the names hard to find.

Instruct your guests to look for the names and to guess where else these friends can be found.

A	S	T	S	O	V	E	S
M	A	R	I	A	E	T	O
D	R	O	M	L	R	R	T
A	E	K	E	E	N	A	O
M	M	R	I	A	D	C	H
Y	E	A	N	M	L	I	Z

Find these names in the puzzle:
AMY, MARIA, LIZ, SARAH, KIM, TRACI

Where else can you look for these friends?

On the inside...

Give information about the party. Instruct your guests to bring a wrapped party favor.

At a "Just Because We're Friends" party on (date/time) at (your address)

Please bring a wrapped party favor that relates to the theme of friendship.

PARTY DECORATIONS

Familiar Faces
Hang paper doll chains with photos or drawings of your guests' faces.

Matching Hearts
Think of famous friendly pairs, such as Charlie Brown and Linus. For each pair, make a paper heart and cut it in half. Write one name on each half. Then hang the halves around the room and challenge your guests to find matching pairs.

Friendship Flowers
Use chrysanthemums, the official flowers of friendship, as a centerpiece.

Fun and Games

These great games are sure to get your guests giggling!

Friendship Knot

The object of this game is to join together—and then figure out how to get yourselves apart. It's harder than you think!

1 Stand in a circle and put your hands into the center.

2 Grab onto each other's hands. BUT, you can't hold the hand of the person right next to you. AND, you and another person can't hold both hands.

3 Once the group is in a knot, everyone will have to work together to get untangled!

Hint: **Instead of each person shouting directions and moving around at the same time, take turns suggesting what to do and how to move next.**

Musical Favors

Make passing out favors much more fun with this combination of musical chairs and hot potato.

1 Gather all the guests into a circle. Get out the wrapped party favors that everyone was asked to bring.

2 Pass the favors around and around in the circle while a parent or older sibling plays some music. Keep going until the music stops.

3 When the music is turned off, the gift each guest is holding is hers to keep!

83

Serve Surprising Cupcakes

What could be a sweeter treat than finding a friendly message at the bottom of a cupcake? Mix up a batch for your fabulous friends!

You Will Need:

- Cupcake papers
- Muffin tin
- Your favorite cake mix
- Baking tools needed to prepare the cake mix
- Frosting and cake decorations
- Birthday candles

You are a great friend.

1 Line the muffin tin with cupcake papers.

2 For each cupcake, write a friendly greeting on another piece of cupcake paper and fold it tightly into a little square. Place 1 folded note in each cup in the tin.

Food for Thought

Give your friends one of these messages to chew on:

U R A Q T
("You are a cutie")

voy era a doog dneirf
("You are a good friend" spelled backwards)

I ♥ 2 B with U
("I love to be with you")

U R Gr8
("You are great")

3 With an adult, prepare the cake mix according to the directions on the package. Then pour the batter into the cups, covering the notes. Fill each cup about halfway.

4 Have an adult help you bake the cupcakes according to the directions. When cool, frost each cupcake with your own flair!

5 Put a candle in each cupcake. When it's time to serve the cupcakes, light the candles. Have everyone sing "Happy Friends' Day to Us!" and blow out the candles.

A Friendship to Sing About!

Finish the party on a high note with some songs about friends. Try the ones below or make up your own songs.

Sung to the tune of *America*

(The song that begins "My country 'tis of thee...")

My friends mean lots to me,

They're special as can be.

They always care!

<u>(Something you all love)</u> we adore,

<u>(Something you all hate)</u> we ignore!

But that's what friends are for . . .

We always share!

Sung to the tune of Row, Row, Row Your Boat

(Guest's name) , (2nd guest's name)

(3rd guest's name) , and (4th guest's name)

Are all my (adjective) friends,

We love to (verb) , (another verb) , and (another verb) ,

Together till the end!

Sung as guests leave, to the tune of On Top of Old Smoky

At (name of host) 's party,

We had lots of fun.

We played (name of game) ,

Which (name of winner) won.

We ate lots of food,

The (name of food) tasted great.

It's time to go home, friends.

It's getting real late!

FRIENdSHIp FiLE

Every good friend deserves a place in your heart—and a page in this book! Cut photos of your friends to fit in the frames. Then fill in all the information and have your friends add their personal autographs.

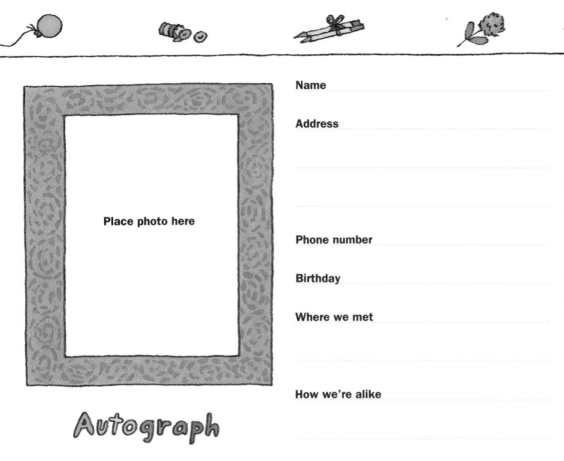

Place photo here

Autograph

Name ....

Address ....

....

....

Phone number ....

Birthday ....

Where we met ....

....

How we're alike ....

....

....

How we're different ....

....

....

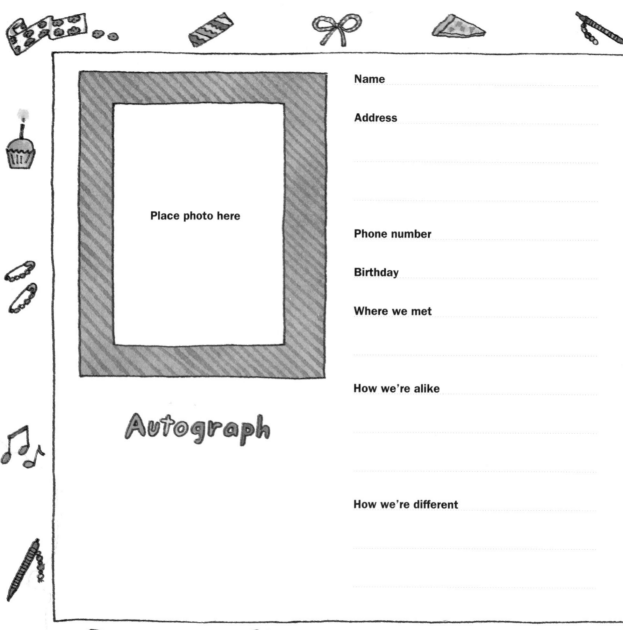

Place photo here

Autograph

Name

Address

Phone number

Birthday

Where we met

How we're alike

How we're different

Place photo here

Autograph

Name

Address

Phone number

Birthday

Where we met

How we're alike

How we're different

Place photo here

Autograph

Name ....

Address ....

....

....

Phone number ....

Birthday ....

Where we met ....

....

How we're alike ....

....

....

How we're different ....

....

....

Place photo here

Autograph

Name

Address

Phone number

Birthday

Where we met

How we're alike

How we're different

Place photo here

Name ....

Address ....

....

....

....

Phone number ....

Birthday ....

Where we met ....

....

How we're alike ....

....

....

How we're different ....

....

Autograph

When you get your **FREE** catalogue, you'll see that it's true. It's full of fun things for American girls like you.

B*ooks, dolls, dresses, and other delights* *that bring the past*

alive. Great new mix & match A.G.Gear™ *for school, sports, play, and every day!*

 Dolls that look just like you because you're a *part of history, too.*

Bitty Baby® *An adorable baby doll, a bitty bear, little books,* *and tiny toys to share.*

To get your FREE catalogue, call 1-800-845-0005.
American Girl, 8400 Fairway Place, Middleton, WI 53562

AmericanGirl™

12948